GROWING TOGETHER

How to plan all-age learning in the Church

edited by

Megan Coote

The Joint Board of Christian Education
Melbourne

Published by
THE JOINT BOARD OF CHRISTIAN EDUCATION
Second Floor, 10 Queen Street, Melbourne 3000, Australia

GROWING TOGETHER
How to plan all-age learning in the Church
© The Joint Board of Christian Education 1988

Acknowledgement: This book is a revision of **Planning for Growing Together** which was written by Rob Evans and published by JBCE in 1980.

National Library of Australia
Cataloguing-in-Publication entry.
Growing together: how to plan all-age learning in the Church.
ISBN 0 85819 644 1.
1. Intergenerational Christian education. I. Joint Board of Christian Education. II. Coote, Megan 1932-   . III. Evans, Rob. Planning for growing together. IV. Title: Planning for growing together.
268'.6

First printed 1988.

Design: Liz Sharp
Typeset: JBCE
Printer: Brown Prior Anderson Pty Ltd

JB88/1445

Contents

	Page
What is all-age learning?	6
What all-age learning offers	8
Different ways of being together for all-age learning	9
The basic all-age learning pattern	10
All-age worship-learning programs	13
Church-family day	15
Church-family camp	16
Clusters	18
How to get started in all-age learning	19
Developing your own program	21
Planning your session	26
A smorgasbord of program ideas	27
The use of stories in all-age learning	43
Idea starters	45

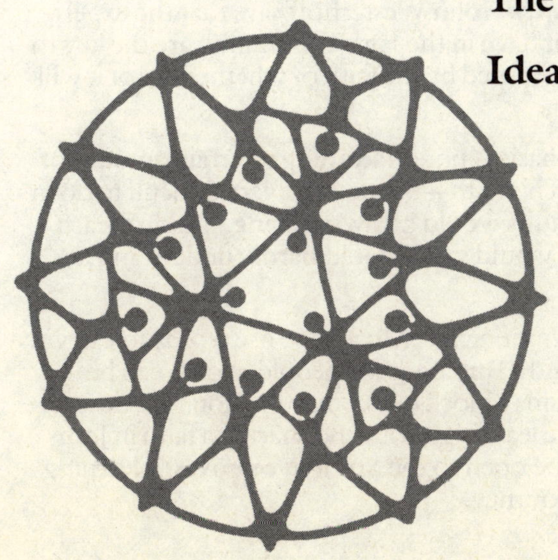

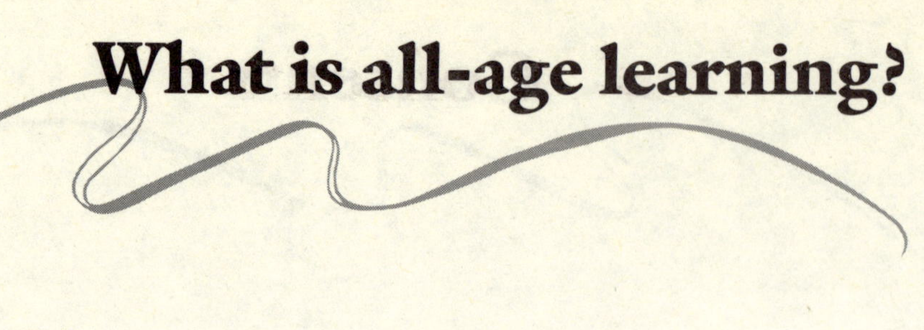

All-age learning (sometimes called 'inter-generational learning') involves children, youth and adults TOGETHER in learning.

● It affirms that adults may learn with and from children and youth, just as children and youth may learn with and from adults.

● It acknowledges the importance of gathering three generations together — so that the idealism and vision of the future-oriented generation can be tempered with the memory and experience of the past — in order that together we may take responsible action in the present.

● All-age learning doesn't just happen. It takes hard work to share your ideas, your feelings and your faith — in fact yourself with others.

● All-age learning is the active sharing of faith experiences across the generations.

● All-age learning has an important place as a supplement to age-graded learning. It does not replace the important learning that happens in children's, youth or adult groups. Rather, it adds a new dimension to learning in the faith community.

Another and more subtle characteristic of all-age learning has to do with the nature of learning and the nature of the faith community.

In *Values for tomorrow's children*, John Westerhoff says that the experiences people have or do not have in the faith community are the key to whether or not they will be grasped by the faith or whether or not it will have any meaning for them.

In all-age learning the emphasis is not on learning a certain amount of information about the church's faith — something very difficult to do in an all-age setting. Either adults would go away saying, 'I didn't learn anything new'; or children would say, 'I could hardly understand a thing.'

There are many ways to communicate. Mostly we use words to carry our thoughts, feelings or faith. But for some people, words can be confusing and limiting and may block our communiction. We need to remind ourselves that we are learning about and sharing a faith in Jesus Christ. We are learning to be open to the Spirit in our lives, a learning which is in itself a lifetime journey.

In all-age learning the emphasis is upon making opportunities to experience vital, living faith. All ages can learn from such an experience; drawing from it at their own levels of maturity. While the content of faith is important, so are opportunities for encounters with persons who are living the life of faith.

As you read through the stories and program ideas in this manual, you will see that it is about people of all ages coming together to share their lives and faith in many different ways and settings.

All-age learning is not new. It was happening in the Hebrew family when the father repeated the faith story in response to his son's question (Deuteronomy 6:20-25). What is new is that all-age learning is being used as one part of the formal learning program of the church — the family of faith.

What all-age learning offers

There are few churches who could not take advantage of what all-age learning has to offer. Among its possibilities are:

● An opportunity for the church to be what it claims to be — a community for all ages.

● An opportunity for each person to explore ideas, concepts, themes in such a way that it gives meaning to life.

● An opportunity for parents and children to learn from each other.

● An opportunity to discover and appreciate the rich variety of gifts and needs of people of all ages. (This is less likely in small age-graded groups).

● An opportunity for family members to grow in their understanding and support for one another.

In all-age learning the door is opened for opportunities for a fresh dimension of *joy* and *celebration* and a vision of the Spirit in action.

Different ways of being together for all-age learning

How to choose the model that is right for you and your congregation

Many churches are coming together in a variety of ways for all-age learning. Each way needs to be considered on the basis of local church needs, purposes and available resources.

Four patterns can be distinguished, though there is some blending between the patterns and variations within each.

1. The basic all-age learning pattern (page 10)

2. All-age worship-learning programs (page 13)

3a. Church-family day (page 15)

3b. Church-family camp (page 16)

4. Clusters (page 18)

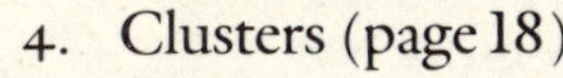

1. The basic all-age learning pattern

How it began

After the rush to be on time, the first thing to catch one's eye was the huge calendar with the months of November and December featured.

However, first things first. There were leaders inviting us to make our own name tag, we could decorate it with something to do with Christmas.

As our name tags were finished we were invited to write up on the calendar the dates and events we have 'booked up' for this Advent season.

I knew things got hectic around Christmas time, but to see that calendar, my goodness, how do we all survive?

We talked about it in small groups and even the children seem to be 'on the go'.

Listening time

We were invited to sit down, the seats were not arranged in rows, but so we could see each other and the different things that were happening out the front.

There were two people standing at microphones.

One told us the story of Luke 1:26-38 in a strong sure voice. At the same time from the other microphone a really frantic harassed voice read of the list of events from the calendar we had just filled in.

It was interesting to hear the sure voice of Luke's message that was almost drowned out in patches by the other harassed voice, but still underneath I was conscious of the Bible message.

Then we were given some...

Activities to choose from

to help us think some more about Advent.

PAINTING ON THE WINDOWS OF THE HALL   I'd always wanted to put some life and colour into this old hall. We were surprised to find there are plastic paints just for that purpose and it will peel off later if need be. Some of us talked for a few minutes about what was important to paint on those windows where all would see. What did we really want to say?

CICADAS AND ADVENT.   I had never associated
cicadas with advent before. (See story) I wondered
what that group would be doing.

CICADAS AND ADVENT
by Rev. Lloyd Shirley

'What is that noise in the trees we hear each night?' the
visitors from England asked. They were talking about the high
pitched rasping noise which can sometimes be so loud and
constant on hot nights that it becomes quite annoying. The
insect which makes the sound is not easy to see because it
hides itself amongst the leaves of the tree. It is called a cicada
(s'kah-da), a winged insect up to about 10 cm long. By using
two rounded flaps which cover two hollow spaces under his
body the male cicada makes the noise to call a female cicada to
him. Sometimes a male cicada waits up to eleven years for this
time to come.

The life of the male cicada begins when his mother cuts a slit in
the tree bark and lays her eggs there. When the tiny cicadas
come out from these eggs they let go of the twig and fall to
the ground. Then they make a hole in the ground and dig their
way to the tree roots and live on the sap they suck from the
roots. Their hard skins keep them safe. A long time later —
sometimes as long as eleven years — a time comes for the
cicada to come up from under the ground into the light. Great
changes are ahead! Digging its way to the open air it climbs a
tree or fence and then waits. Something wonderful is going to
happen! The skin on its back splits and slowly the new cicada,
ready for new life, leaves the old skin behind. Green blood
pumps through its wings to make them stiff and strong. A few
hours later the male cicada flies up into a tree and hides in the
leaves to sing a song for a mate. A long wait — but a different
life ahead!

At Advent we are waiting for something to happen. We wait
for the time of Jesus' birth and look for ways to let him change
our lives. Think about how Mary may have felt while waiting
for Jesus' birth. Talk about the new and different kinds of
people we can become when we trust Jesus. Are there ways
in which he wants us to change and become new people?

AN ADVENT TREE   Some people made an advent
tree from green transparent 'contact'. A large one for
a large window or a small one on overhead projector
transparency sheets for individuals to take home.
Each week we added a symbol representing something from worship on that day.

One of the groups decided they would like to make a
large tree and encase it, put a spotlight on it and put it
where the local community could see it.

As we talked some more about what Advent and
Christmas means to us we realised how little impact
we have on the community around us. These are the
thoughts that came to me —

'I would like our family to talk about our own plans
for Christmas. I think there are things I would like to
change this year.

One thing I have discovered is how little I really
know the other people in this church. This event has
helped me to get to know people better — especially
the children. We always say Christmas is for children.
I've learnt again this morning it is for us all.'

AGAPE MEAL   We came together for a sharing
time and an agape meal. (An agape meal is a Christian
gathering to express the Koinonia — the community, sharing, fellowship — of the 'family of
God'.)

The leader held up an egg timer, and as we watched
the grains of sand falling through I marvelled at the
millions of grains of sand; the millions of people in
the world and the fact that God cares about us all.

We joined in a brief closing. The minister began

Leader: We join together waiting again for the gift
of Jesus Christ.

People: Because of that gift we give our love and
gifts to each other.

Leader: We now share our gift of food as a symbol
of Jesus coming among us.

People: Thank you Jesus, for showing us how to
love.

The children helped by distributing Christmas
biscuits to everyone.

It really felt like I was part of a faith community.

Who participates?

Usually there are no restrictions placed on participation. The use of the word 'family' is discouraged as
this tends to isolate persons who do not think of
themselves as being part of a family i.e. singles.

Allowance needs to be made for occasional peer
groupings within the overall all-age structures. This
is particularly important for young people and for
those for whom the possibility of change may be
difficult. A choice of activities is important. People
usually invest more of themselves in something they
have chosen.

The participation of very young children may be
limited by their attention span and language skills.
Their participation may be encouraged by parents or
other adults interpreting and helping their children.

In other situations 'opt out' activity centres are provided for the very young. Such centres have play
dough or crayons and paper or soft toys. Pictures on
the theme can help introduce ideas to the children for
their activities. Young children 'soak up' more than
adults realise by being part of all-age activities in
this way.

What happens?

The program printed here was one used for a major Christian festival (Advent). Other festivals (Easter, Pentecost), local church festivals (anniversaries, spring, thanksgiving), offer good material about which to develop a program. Pages 21 ff. provide more suggestions. A segment 'just for fun' is sometimes worth including.

Who leads?

Good leadership is a key to the success of all-age programs. However, one value of such programs is that they develop and use a wider range of leadership skills.

While it is important to encourage as many as possible to be part of the leadership team, it is also important to allow people the freedom to decline such an invitation until they are ready to be involved in this way.

Among the skills needed for leadership are organisational ability, educational and theological insight, enthusiasm and creativity. Being part of the leadership group can provide the opportunity for learning and 'getting to know' other members better. It is good to include children and young people in the planning.

Other helpers are often needed for the various activities chosen and these people need to be invited well beforehand so adequate preparation time may be given.

Where does it take place?

The types of activities chosen generally require space for the movement of people and for groups to work together. This means flexible seating arrangements. Proximity to work-space and kitchens is desirable if a meal is part of the program. Most church halls are adaptable for such use.

When does it take place?

No one time has evolved as being 'right' for all-age learning. Many churches find Sunday a convenient day because the program can be linked with regular public worship. Friday evening over a meal is another time many people find suitable.

Minimising the change to the time of public worship is important if there is difficulty 'fitting in' everything on a Sunday morning. There is still experimenting going on with regard to the frequency of such programs.

2. All-age worship-learning programs

The 'Welcome' sign spoke for itself, while through the glass doors last minute preparations could be seen.

'Sunday at 9' was about to be launched.

The church seats had been moved to form two circles. A young pianist provided some welcoming music.

Four children/young people from the two planning families helped with name tags and offered everybody a glass of water to which was added some fizzy 'fruit saline' powder.

A buzz of conversation could be heard as 60 people of all ages arrived and got settled.

The theme for the program came from the lectionary reading for the day — The Transfiguration.

The order was as follows:

INTRODUCTION AND WELCOME

PRAISE — Hymn 'There's a light upon the mountain' (No. 207 *The Australian Hymn Book/With One Voice*).

SHARING THINGS THAT TRANSFORM — including the transformed water.

SONG 'God loves you' — an action song that included the very small children.

WHAT THE BIBLE TELLS US Luke 9:28-36

OUR MOUNTAIN TOP EXPERIENCES — We were all invited to take a minute or two for quiet reflection. We were asked to identify a mountain top experience. Or a time we have had when everything was so good (terrific/wonderful) that we wished it could go on for ever.

Right across the back of the church was paper with more than enough mountains on it for all of us to write/draw our special time or place. We were invited to talk to two people (preferably of a different generation) about our mountain top.

Some comments from the mountain tops as well as comments on the readings were shared in the whole group.

Very small children were provided for, in a spot of their own, drawing happy times they had enjoyed. All other ages drew/wrote about their mountain top experiences.

CARE AND SHARE Lenten appeal Five projects were chosen to do during Lent and we took the opportunity to hear about them and give to them.

SHARING OUR GIFTS — the offering.

OUR PRAYERS — Our prayers included a responsive prayer 'On Transfiguration Day' from *Australian Prayers* by Bruce Prewer.

SONG — 'One more step along the world I go' from *Songs of Sydney Carter*, Book 4.

The words of this song talk about our journey through life and the chorus goes —
> 'And it's from the old I travel to the new.
> Keep me travelling along with you.'

This summed up our time together. We sang two of the verses and then took hands and moved round the communion table and around the church and out the door to be part of the world.

Who participates?

Worship and learning combined in this way is not for everyone. This needs to be recognised by local church planners from the outset. There are those for whom worship must follow measured liturgical patterns and forms. Others like a hushed stillness and quietness for their worship. That is their choice. However, for others it IS worship and makes possible their participation in the life of the church.

Who leads?

Generally different families or a small group of adults and children/young people take it in turn to lead. **It is important that the minister of the local church** is drawn into the overall planning or leadership in this pattern. The program is then seen to be a legitimate expression of the church's worship and learning and is not seen to be in opposition to other forms of worship within the parish.

Where does it take place?

At times it is possible for the worship location to be used for this type of program. If this is possible, it further helps to legitimate this form of worship and learning. However the fixed seating in many churches is unsuitable for this style of worship-learning. It is important to find a location that encourages involvement of all ages, freedom of movement etc., while still providing opportunity for the group to develop their own liturgical furnishings — a special table, cloth, seating in a circle.

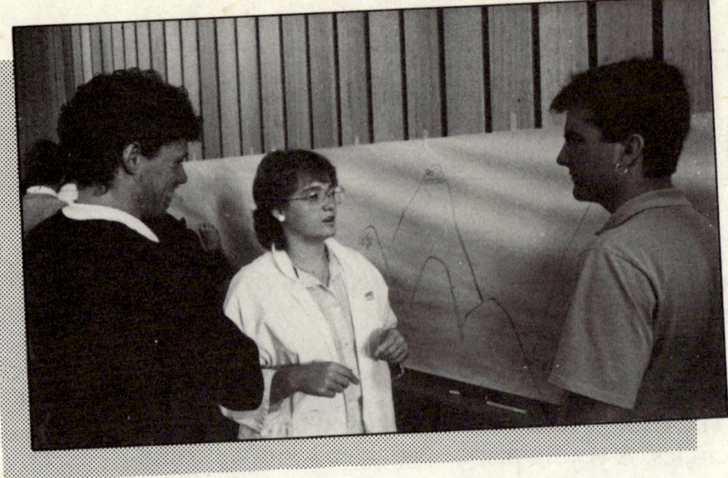

When does it take place?

The usual day is of course, Sunday, but finding a particular time on Sunday often raises difficulties in relation to established programs. No one pattern has emerged. Each local congregation needs to work out what is best for them. Some meet while other forms of worship or learning are taking place; others have to meet at quite inconvenient times so as not to clash in time or location. Both these practices can have unfortunate repercussions. It is important to meet at a time and location that will ensure success (all other things being equal), e.g. if you have a large group of teenagers, 8.30 a.m. on a Sunday is unlikely to work with them

Some groups meet weekly and have done so for many years, while others meet fortnightly or monthly. Care needs to be taken where a group meets monthly that the momentum keeps the group going.

This pattern of worship-learning challenges the church to examine a number of the assumptions made about worship and learning, and what constitutes each.

The participation of children in the sacraments is currently under discussion within the Uniting Church in Australia. Following an Assembly decision of 1985, Councils of Elders will be finding ways to include children in the Sacrament of Holy Communion. Books to help in that process are available from the Joint Board of Christian Education.

It is possible to plan a **segment** within the more 'traditional' worship service, e.g. a dramatic reading of the Bible passage or daily newspapers may be distributed for congregational members to find concerns as a basis for prayers of intercession.

3a. Church-family day

A Sunday in summer on board a ferry to Bruny Island

Well, a little windy for summer, but nevertheless approximately 250 people from five congregations within the parish met at the Hobart quay ready to enjoy a day together. To begin the day, as the ferry started its trip down the Derwent river, those on board took part in a service of worship. (A service a little different from usual — as the occasion demanded.) The organ was replaced by trumpet and flute, some informality replaced the more traditional worship. Stories, meditation and dialogue helped people of all ages to make their individual response within the worshipping community.

Once the ferry berthed, there was still four hours before the return journey.

There were games on the beach for all ages together. We took the opportunity to discover the names and something about people not known before. Some groups went off exploring other parts of the island.

Lunch was welcome after the 9 o'clock start.

After lunch 'A walk with our senses' helped us to take more interest in our surroundings. We used our senses of touch, sight, smell, taste and hearing to search out the wonders of God's creation.

We discussed our use of creation; the ways we may continue to co-create or hinder that creation.

Back on board the ferry there was time on the return trip to share some of the discoveries about ourselves, about each other and about God.

Where else?

In some places it is possible to hire a steam train and stay on board all day. A train trip to the country and the use of a property is a real possibility — contact a country church and suggest the idea. Camp and conference centres or national parks are other possibilities for church family days.

What happens?

As with the 'Basic all-age learning pattern' (page 10ff.), the program is planned for all ages to interact at least for the main part of the day. With more time and recreational facilities available there is opportunity for more relaxed and informal learning — as well as learning related to the particular environment. Worship is an important part of the total program.

When does it take place?

Sunday has developed as the time most suitable for a Church-family day. There is a commitment to be part of worship and it is not difficult to extend that time if planning is carried out well beforehand. Arrangements for worship for those who cannot attend are important. A public holiday is also a possibility.

Who leads?

The leadership requirements are much the same as in the 'Basic all-age learning pattern'. Additional helpers may be required for transport and catering.

3b. A Church-family camp

At a conference centre high on the hill overlooking the sea, cars were unloading their passengers. People were calling greetings to each other and trying to find their cabins in the dark. The Conference centre had come alive for the weekend.

Friday night

There was just time to unpack before the Friday evening session began. WE BELONG TOGETHER was the theme for a parish camp held at a Conference centre near the beach.

The gong was sounded at 9 o'clock to bring the eighty people into the hall to begin the weekend program.

What followed was a time to help adults and children to get to know each other a little better.

Those present were placed into 2 circles. Adults on the outside and children and young people on the inside. One circle moved around to music. When the music stopped each pair was asked to talk for one minute about the following : my favourite T.V. program… a favourite place at home… a living person whom I admire… something good that happened to me recently… when I get mad I usually… something I would like to do better… coming down to this camp I felt… (It's not hard to think of others that are not too threatening.)

A brief time of meditation for all ages concluded the evening.

Saturday morning: the body

The Bible reading from 1 Corinthians 12 was used as the basis for the morning's activities. Eighty people of all ages were invited to choose one part of the body from the reading or another part of their own choice. Each group of 6 or 7 people made their part of the body from a wide range of creative materials. Such a conglomeration of odd shapes sizes and materials was a sight to behold!

Assembling the three bodies was a significant time. The reading from 1 Corinthians 12:12-28a was re-written as a dialogue between different parts of the body and the session ended at that point.

After lunch we went for a walk around a large lake. It was **a walk with a difference**. Groups of three or four people were tied to each other by the wrist. It

was a very slippery muddy place. We realised that if one person from a small group slipped into the lake, then all would fall in: or if one slipped in the mud, the other two or three would have to follow. At the end of the walk we cleaned off the mud, cooked marshmallows and reflected about the experience we had just been through. Then followed free time, fun time games and dance time.

Sunday morning

We used a roll of newsprint and drew an outline around the children and young people.* They were asked to print lots of things in the various parts of their body about themselves. Name, age, sex, the things they enjoyed doing, the feelings they had about the weekend, people who are important, times they remembered as being special, places they have been to, holidays they have enjoyed, something about the church and Sunday school or youth group, and any other information they wished. Some of the very young children drew their project. On completion their projects were placed on a wall for all to look at.

At the same time the adults were asked to write a mini view of themselves. Adults and children talked to each other as people thought about what to include. Things from the following list were used as starters: Who were some significant people in your life? What times did you find it difficult to find God? What have been the most significant ways your faith has been nurtured over the years? In what ways would you like your Christian faith to develop over the next 12 months?

During quite a long sharing time we came to know each other much better.

CLOSING WORSHIP

This gathered the thoughts and feelings of the weekend. As we stood in a circle each person took the end of a streamer from the centre of the circle. We were invited to write one gift we had to offer to our church. We closed with the creed from the United Church of Canada (words below) and walked away from our temporary community singing the hymn 'A new commandment I give unto you.' (No. 571 *The Australian Hymn Book/With One Voice*)

A creed from the United Church of Canada

We are not alone, we live in God's world.

We believe in God:

who has created and is creating,

who has come in Jesus, the Word
made flesh, to reconcile
and make new,

who works in us and others
by the Spirit.

We trust in God.

We are called to be the Church:

to celebrate God's presence,

to love and serve others,

to seek justice and resist evil,

to proclaim Jesus, crucified and risen,
our judge and our hope.

In life, in death, in life beyond death,
God is with us.

We are not alone.

Thanks be to God.

All the people found the weekend together a valuable experience, resolving to have another church-family camp in twelve months time.

Who participates?

As for the church-family day the whole church-family is encouraged to participate, but the participation of some will be limited by availability, the location, transport and other personal factors.

What happens?

As with the 'Basic all-age learning pattern', the program is planned for all ages to interact. There is opportunity for more relaxed learning to take place, for time of informal conversation, and more time away from schedules and regular activities.

Who leads?

The leadership requirements are much the same as for the 'basic pattern'. Additional leaders to assist with matters such as transport, catering, cleaning will be necessary. Planning and advertising well in advance is important.

Cost? The cost will vary depending on whether the camp site is fully catered for, or whether the group caters for itself.

* The people who planned this weekend chose one way for the adults and another way for the children to prepare their view of themselves. It is possible if one has the time and space for all to work in the same way.

4. Clusters

The time — Sunday afternoon, 4 p.m. at the Parker's home.

A group of about 20 people had come together for the afternoon program. A happy time of conversation, greeting and play was taking place between people of several generations.

It was almost Easter so that was the theme for the program.

David called for everyone to gather round so the organised activities could begin.

A GAME with two teams of mixed ages was the first activity. The props were hard boiled eggs and some sticks, with an extra supply of hard boiled eggs.

The race was a relay and the object was to get as many eggs to each end of the large family room as possible. There was no real winner, but lots of laughter over broken eggs, and time for reflection. People talked about new life, hope, breaking free like the little bird that has to break free from its shell and finally Jesus breaking free from the tomb on Easter Sunday.

Then followed SHARING TIME, (initiated by the leader for the day) again with two groups of mixed ages. They were all asked to complete the unfinished sentence. 'When I think of Easter I think of…'

Each group made a collage from the completed sentences. As well as the usual scissors, glue, magazines and material scraps, the bush was near enough for one group to make a rough wooden cross that took the centre of the collage.

The collages were hung up on the wall. The group gathered around the collage with the cross and shared in a simple communion. The song 'Let us break bread together' (No 433 *The Australian Hymn Book/With One Voice*) was sung, followed by a simple meditation.

Then came MEAL TIME and HOME at 6.30 p.m.

Some more about clusters

The model most used in Australia has been adapted from the model pioneered by Margaret Sawin of U.S.A. A cluster consists of four or five family units who meet together over a period of time (a minimum of twelve sessions), for shared learning experiences. The questions and concerns of everyday life form the basis for the session. It is not a therapy group.

In the American model a cluster would be led by a team of two specially trained leaders. This does make a difference to the type of programs and the themes covered.

In Australia and New Zealand clusters it is more likely that the cluster will be led by people from within the cluster itself. The practice of different families taking the leadership in turn is common.

When and where?

● The program detailed here is fairly typical of most clusters. The times may be slightly different, but a meal is always an important part of the program.

● Private homes mostly provide the venue for clusters. If the occasion demands it a church hall with suitable catering facilities may be used.

Who is in it?

Generally a cluster involves four to six families (making about 24 persons in all). A family unit may be a nuclear family, a single person or grandparent(s). The families 'contract' together to meet for a specified period of time and for a particular purpose. The 'contract' may be quite formal, being prepared by the families meeting together with everyone signing, or less formal and referred to as a general 'understanding' or 'agreement' that the families have about their purpose.

What else can clusters do?

● It is fairly common for a cluster to be involved in at least one camp a year.

● The cluster group written up in this section also had occasional study groups for the adults, but that was a separate activity from the cluster.

How to get started in all-age learning

Be positive!

All age learning has much to offer the local church (see page 8). What it offers is for building up the life of the local church and not for tearing down all that was done in the past. **Hence begin by emphasising what all-age learning offers.** Not all all-age programs are a panacea for ailing programs. If the Sunday school is dying for lack of leadership, an all-age program is not necessarily the answer. It, too, may die in infancy for the same reason.

Start in a small way!

All age learning seems new to many people, so begin by giving people a taste of it. Whet their appetites for more. This can be done by introducing activities which could be used in an all-age program into existing programs from time to time.

This has the advantage of helping others to understand and appreciate what you are so enthusiastic about, and gives you the opportunity to learn how best to use all-age activities. You could try one event like a Christian festival or a local church anniversary. Evaluate this before attempting more.

Change by addition

There are enough difficulties in trying to set up a new program without having to cope with the difficulties that arise from the loss of other programs.
So in the first instance, set up the all-age program as an optional new program.

Who makes the decisions?

In most churches there is a Council of elders or Christian education committee or a similar group that makes the final decision.

It is crucial to have the support of the minister and whichever group or committee it is that makes the decisions. How best can you share your dream with them? It is likely that your Denomination's Christian Education Department or its equivalent will have some details of churches that are involved in all-age learning. Go and visit and talk to those groups where they are close enough for you to do this.

Write to them if visiting is out of the question. Allow yourself plenty of time for the initial investigations as well as sufficient time to win support, make the decision and implement that decision.

Win support

This is implied in a number of comments already made. It is, however, so important that it must be said separately too. Ask yourself and those with whom you are working

● Who are the people who will be affected by the new program?

● In what ways can these people benefit from the program?

● In what ways can they lose?

● What are the implications of the time and place you are suggesting for the all-age learning program?

● Who will be the leaders?

● To whom will they be responsible/accountable?

● How will the minister be involved?

YOU'RE SET TO GO, you have planned to have an initial program, once a month for 6 months. Great. You have also arranged an evaluation at the end of that time. Now learn more about the do's and dont's of all-age learning or all-age worship/learning.

Before you start

Look at your total learning program again as it relates to the all-age program you have chosen. Are changes necessary? Are there gaps in your program? Can they be filled? If so, how?

The above comments apply to the other models of all-age activities described on pages 13, 15, 16 and 18.

Developing your own program

Planning and conducting one or two all-age programs is comparatively easy, the hard part is to KEEP GOING.

Enthusiasm keeps one going for a time and then it really is HARD WORK and COMMITMENT that keeps groups going month after month and year after year.

There is no substitute for careful planning and evaluation.

These pointers will help you along the way.

1. GOALS are an important first step. What do you want to achieve in your group? Jot down your ideas.

2. You will probably have in mind a particular type of program. Check again that your choice fits your particular situation (see page 25).

3. RESOURCES are many and varied. The most important resources are the people themselves, and the opportunity given for interaction and sharing together across the ages. Having said that, there are specific resources that need to be identified —

● LEADERS for small groups and for particular activities. These people will need to clearly understand the goals.

● THE PLACE is also important to enable people to mix together in small groups and for certain activities to be undertaken without worrying about the best carpet becoming stained.

● FURNITURE AND EQUIPMENT are other essentials, e.g. overhead projector, the usual supplies of newsprint, felt-tip pens, crayons, paper, cardboard, paint and brushes, glue, old newspapers and magazines.

4. NOW FOR THE PROGRAM ITSELF. You may have gained some ideas from the previous pages. The first essential is to select the THEME. Think carefully about your prospective group and choose the theme that seems most appropriate to their present needs (see pages 26ff.).

A checklist for planning your all-age event

Up to this point you have done your homework well! You have researched the various models for all-age learning through reading, talking to others and maybe visiting or writing to people involved in similar programs in other places.

You have won support, thought carefully about the implications of the program, the place, the time and the involvement of all ages together. Now you are ready to try your own wings.

This checklist is designed to help you with some basic details.

1. It is tempting to want to cover a lot of territory during the time you have. Resist this temptation. There is only so much that can be effectively covered in one hour or the duration of the event. It is better to keep it simple especially at first and follow the theme right through. There will be other occasions to uncover further exciting truths.

2. Who will be on the planning team? Are there people with experience that you can team with those keen to learn?

3. Check that all the planning team members are familiar with the aims and purpose of the event.

4. Will additional helpers be needed for the session?

5. What will be the relationship of the learning event (if that is what you are planning) to your regular congregational worship?

6. Have you made an estimate of the numbers of people you can reasonably expect to participate?

7. How will the event be publicised? e.g. invitations, posters, church notices etc.

8. What equipment and supplies will you need? and how much or how many of particular things? e.g. name tags, felt pens, paper, card, what size etc.

9. Is there sufficient clarity on length of event, location, time?

10. Have the necessary buildings been booked? (hall, rooms, kitchen)

11. Evaluation is an important part of all-age programs. An evaluation needs to be completed by those who attend the event and those members of the planning team. (See simple evaluation form below.)

12. How will you share the findings with church councils and planners of future events?

A simple evaluation form

Would you please help us to improve this program by completing the following:

What I liked best was ....

....

What I learned was ....

....

What I would change would be ....

There is no need to
sign your name, but your age would help for future planning events.   My age is ....

Report to local church

A report to your local church authority could include some of the information below. It is helpful to pass on more of the detail to the planning team for the next all-age event.

1. The reaction of the leadership team to the program was...

2. The reactions of participants to the program were...

3. In relation to the goals of the program we believe people learnt...

4. We as leaders learnt...

5. As we look back on the program, we would offer the following comments upon...
   - our leadership and preparation
   - the participants, number and ages
   - the resources
   - the number of sessions, date and time
   - the location
   - the furniture and equipment
   - the publicity, promotion and support for the program
   - the link with worship
   - the relationships of the program to other programs (e.g. Sunday school)

6. Our recommendations for the future are...

7. The program summary:

<table>
<tr><td>The theme was ...</td><td></td></tr>
<tr><td>There were .... adults</td><td>Number of sessions held on ....(date)</td></tr>
<tr><td>......... young people and children involved.</td><td>.........................(time)</td></tr>
<tr><td></td><td>..................(location)</td></tr>
<tr><td>The leaders were ...</td><td></td></tr>
<tr><td>Overall the program was ...</td><td></td></tr>
</table>

Categories for planning all-age events

George Koehler offers some help in his book *Learning Together* (Discipleship Resources, Nashville). He has devised a worksheet of over fifty learning activities under five different headings. He himself admits that most of the activities could be listed under several categories. However as a way of bringing ideas to the surface the categories are useful.

1. His first list is of activities which help in **deepening relationships with other people.** These activities are particularly important for groups where people don't know one another, or at the beginning of a program to help people to open up communication with one another about the theme, or where large numbers of people are involved in the program. These are activities which help build a team-spirit, a community, from what might have been just a collection of people.

2. Then come activities for **exploring facts, ideas and meanings.** These are the activities which help us to get an overall picture of the theme.

3. The next group of activities is to provide opportunities **for expressing attitudes, beliefs and opinions.** It is in this section that opportunity needs to be given for all ages to express themselves in a variety of ways. It is all too easy for adults to use words to hide real thought and feelings. We need to listen to and learn from children. The care with which we enable adults to use concrete images is an important art in working with all-age groups. Jesus' use of parables is well worth recalling.

4. and 5. The final two lists provide possibilities for learnings to be expressed in action — in **celebrating faith and life** and in activities for **helping people move into Christian discipleship.** Not all forms of responsible Christian action are suitable for children, but we are beginning to see that, given support and opportunity, there are more ways in which children can act than we have often allowed them to do.

When we talk about wanting to make some changes in our lives, whether child or adult it is important to provide the opportunity for support for each other in maintaining some particular stance. It is difficult to maintain a struggle for justice in a particular field without support from someone of like mind.

It is not always necessary to use an activity from every section. Think about your goals, the theme you have chosen and the time available to you. Activities from category 1 are important if your group is large or if it is early days for all-age programs in your area.

It is possible to use the lists to develop a more substantial program, e.g. a church-family camp, with getting-to-know activities on Friday evening, a time for study and research on Saturday morning. Sunday would allow time for worship and taking responsible action.

1. **For deepening relationships with other people**
- conversation in two's and three's
- eating together
- interviewing one another
- nametag making
- non-verbal communication
- sharing family trees
- sharing prized possessions
- symbol sharing
- values clarification (shared)
- walking together

2. **For exploring facts, ideas, meanings**
- Bible study
- cartoon viewing
- comparing hymns or songs
- educational game
- film viewing
- magazine or newspaper search
- opinion poll, survey or census
- paraphrasing
- resource person
- story telling

3. **For expressing attitudes, beliefs, opinions**
- banner making
- caption writing
- collage

- display
- life-line
- painting (brush, cotton ball, crayon, finger, spatter…)
- photography
- poetry (cinquain, free, haiku, jingle, limerick, psalm…)
- poster making
- puppets

4. For celebrating faith and life

- costumes
- creative movement and dancing
- drama (mime, tableau, play…)
- flying kites
- music (band, orchestra, recording, voice…)
- picnic
- reading (antiphonal, choral, echo, responsive…)
- rituals, traditions
- singing
- worship

5. For helping people move into Christian discipleship

- covenant, contract or certificate
- gift making and giving
- news sheet preparation and distribution
- petitions
- planting
- poster or placard
- role playing
- telegramming
- visiting
- witnessing

List adapted from *Learning Together* by George Koehler, p.65
Copyright 1977 by Discipleship Resources. Used by permission of
Discipleship Resources, P.O. Box 840, Nashville, Tn. 37202.

Planning your session

The following pages are intended to aid you in choosing themes and learning activities.

There are two sections

1. A variety of activities on eleven themes (based on George Koehler's categories — pages 29-42).

2. Ideas starters — pages 45-54.

A smorgasbord of program ideas

Contributions by Megan Coote, Jan Hartley and June Wright.

Using the pattern suggested in the previous section, select ideas from among the activities to develop your own programs.

Activities about Advent and Christmas

1. For deepening relationships with other people

Name tags

In two and threes, talk about your own names — their meanings, why selected by parents, nicknames and how these came to be given. Then make name tags for one another. (This can lead on to discussion of Jesus' names.)

Family traditions

In small groups, talk about your own favourite family Christmas traditions. Bring tree decorations, crib sets, special greeting cards etc. to show and arrange into a display.

2. For exploring facts, ideas, meanings

Christmas story books

Make a display of these. Many families treasure an illustrated book about the Christmas story, or they could be encouraged to buy one. In small groups, choose a book to read together and discuss. Which is the best picture? What is the baby called? Why?

The naming of Jesus

Give each small group a Bible passage which refers to the naming of Jesus or his descriptive titles. With the help of the groups, list these names on newsprint, adding meanings where unclear. The names tell us something about the needs and longings of the people who used them. What do they tell? Are our needs and longings in any way the same? In what ways? What do the names tell us about Jesus?

(See Isaiah 40:10-11; Isaiah 42:1-4; Matthew 1:18-23; Matthew 2:1-6; Mark 1:1-3 or 1-12; Luke 1:26-38; Luke 2:8-12; Luke 2:25-32; John 1:1-18.)

Worksheet

Provide worksheets along the lines of the sample given here. Work in pairs, young and old together, to fill in the spaces.

The four weeks before Christmas are called ....
(Advent). This means 'coming'. In these weeks we
prepare for the coming of .... (Jesus). The
prophets were the first to tell of God's ....
(promises) to send a saviour... and so on.

3. For expressing attitudes, beliefs, opinions

Tree of life

Have a large green branch in a pot or a green tree cut
from coloured paper or drawn on newsprint and
attached to a wall. Give out felt pens and circles of
white or brightly coloured card about 150 mm dia-
meter. The cards are to be decorated with words
and/or pictures showing what we consider important
as we get ready for Christmas, for example, Christmas Bowl or Christmas Appeal, family festivities,
carols, Bible verses, pictures of the Bible story, names
of Jesus. Hang cards on the tree.

Sound collage

Allow time in small groups for people to think and
talk in preparation for this activity. For a large group
several tape recorders and microphones will be
needed. Everyone can record on tape something
which he/she believes important about the coming of
Jesus at Christmas. Contributions should be very
brief, e.g. a sentence or two beginning, 'What I believe is...' or 'What I like best is...', several voices
singing a verse of a carol, a short Bible reading. When
complete, play your sound collage.

4. For celebrating faith and life

Song writing and singing

Make up words for an Advent song to a well known
tune such as 'All people that on earth do dwell'. For
this, have four groups each writing one line of eight
beats, on a theme such as the names of Jesus, for
example, Jesus our Saviour, born for us; Jesus,
Emmanuel, God with us. Each group can sing their
own line four times, or you can put the four lines
together to make one verse which all groups sing.
Practise until everyone feels confident, then let it go
and really enjoy the sound and feeling.

Costume parade

Have an assortment of dress-up clothes — striped
towels, curtains, bedspreads, scarves, costume jewel-
lery etc. Work in pairs to prepare for the parade. One
dresses up to represent a character in the Advent-
Christmas story — Isaiah, John the Baptist, Mary,
Joseph, Herod, wise men. The other introduces this
person and explains what he/she believes about Jesus
and the significance of his coming. For instance,
Herod speaks of the Messiah as a threat to his own
rule; Joseph sees Jesus as the promised king born of
David's line. Present the parade with a musical background or intersperse with singing of Advent songs.
singing of Advent songs.

5. For helping people move into Christian discipleship

Voting on Christmas observance

Believing that Jesus is God with us as our Saviour
and King should affect the way we celebrate Christmas. In buzz groups, discuss what this means for
you. Then on newsprint, make a list of ideas for
properly celebrating Christmas. Leave space beside
each item where people can register votes for the
ideas they personally could put into practice, for
example, support for Christmas Bowl and Christmas
Appeal.

Prepare for Christmas

More than a time of waiting, Advent is for active
preparation, so have a working bee to tidy the church
grounds, clean church windows, walls and floors,
polish furniture and brasses. If close to Christmas,
put up and decorate a Christmas tree. Then assemble
in the clean building to prepare your hearts and
minds. Sing carols and pray. Meditate on a Bible
passage such as Isaiah 35, or 40:1-11, the leader helping people relax and picture in their minds the scenes
and people that are described and commit themselves
to receive the Lord who came and who is coming.

Activities about Easter (Emmaus)

1. For deepening relationships with other people

Conversations about loss and grief

In groups of four to six people (adults, youth and children in each group wherever possible), talk about times when you have experienced a sense of loss or grief — a family death, death of a pet, loss of an important game or competition. Relate this to the disciples after Jesus' death.

Name tags

Make name tags adding your dream or wish for the world at this Easter time in writing or by drawing.

2. For exploring facts, ideas, meanings

Miming the Bible story

In small groups, ask one of the members who is a good reader to read Luke 24:13-35, noting where this story occurs in the Easter sequence of events. Then assign characters from the story to the group members and ask them to mime their particular part while the passage is re-read.

Make a timeline

Using Bibles, prepare a timeline to show the Easter events and where the Emmaus story fits in. Have plenty of large sheets of paper available. Using felt-tip pens or crayons have everyone illustrate the events on the timeline.

3. For expressing attitudes, beliefs, opinions

Fingerpainting

Do fingerpainting, making use of colour and patterns to convey the changes in the two — as they walked together; then met Jesus; when they realised who he was and understood the meaning of all that had happened; and finally when they shared their excitement and joy with the disciples in Jerusalem.

Banner making

Make banners, expressing the sense of discovery and joy that Cleopas and his friend must have felt as they shared with Jesus and then with the disciples in Jerusalem. Old sheets or coloured burlap can be used for the background of the banners. Provide scraps of material, cord, cotton wool etc., a glue suitable for use with fabrics, scissors and paper for working out patterns.

4. For celebrating faith and life

Sing and dance

Use 'They set out on their homeward road' (*Songs for Worship* No. 37). Start sadly and build up to a crescendo of joy and confidence as the verses progress. Some people may prefer to sing while others dance, or they can do both.

Holy Communion

Share in Holy Communion according to your church's tradition to recall Jesus' appearance to the two when he broke bread with them at Emmaus. Incorporate the words of the Bible reading where appropriate.

Sentence prayers

Write sentence prayers for those people who are saddened or grieving at some loss and who need to know that Jesus is with them. Younger children could draw a picture instead. There is no need for the names of people to be made known. Place the prayers in a bowl on the communion table. The prayers could be used as part of the church's intercessions.

Singing

Join in the round 'Are not our hearts burning within us?' (*Hi God 2*).

5. For helping persons move into Christian discipleship

Interviews

Several people who have felt Jesus' presence with them in a number of different ways in their lives at some time (for example, reading their Bible or a book, or perhaps in a crisis situation) and who have come into a new relationship with God and a deepened understanding of the faith could be interviewed perhaps using a recorder.

Visiting

Plan to visit people who are lonely or in need, not only in the church, but in the wider community. Discuss how you could help them to know that Jesus is risen.

Gift-giving

Give your name tag to another person — encourage the younger to give their name tag to an older person and vice versa. When you give your name tag away, talk about the dream or wish for the world you wrote on your tag at the start of the program.

Closing

Move around greeting people whom you meet and saying, 'The Lord is risen' to which they can respond, 'He is risen indeed.'

Activities about The Kingdom of God

1. For deepening relationships with other people

Viewing a display

Provide a display of items and pictures on the theme of 'Kingdom' for example, pictures of kings and queens, castles — travel poster and some children's books are good sources, a box of jewels, etc. As people arrive, invite them to look at the display and share their comments with someone else. Some people may have lived in a country where a king a queen resides; others may have actually seen a castle or been close to the royal family when on tour. Then in small groups, talk about what a kingdom is. Make sure all the children have a chance to contribute their ideas.

If I were a King/Queen

On a sheet of newsprint mounted on the wall write 'If I were a King/Queen I would…' Ask people to draw a picture/s of what they would do to change the world. Then have them move around silently viewing one another's pictures. Then allow time for talking to one another about their pictures.

2. For exploring facts, ideas, meanings

A 'treasure chest'

Prepare a box to look like a treasure chest. Place in the box items which represent some of Jesus' parables of the Kingdom. Attach to each a piece of paper with the appropriate Bible reference given. For example, some weeds — Matthew 13:24-30, a packet of seeds — Matthew 13:31-32, a packet of yeast — Matthew 13:33, a string of pearls — Matthew 13:45-46, a piece of (fishing) net — Matthew 13:47 and on the 'treasure chest' itself — Matthew 13:44. Divide up into sufficient groups for each of the Bible references you have used. Ask a person from each group to dip into

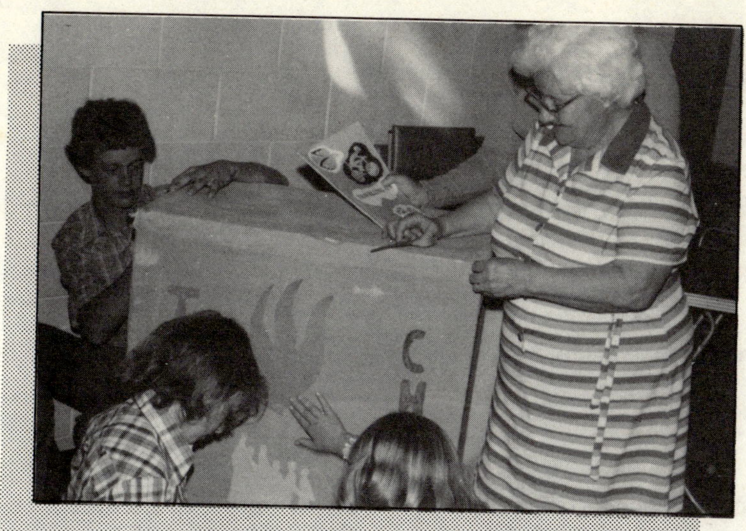

the 'treasure chest' and take an article from it giving the 'treasure chest' to the last group. Then have each group look up the Bible reference and prepare a one sentence statement about why the Kingdom of God is like their particular object. Have each group in turn stand before everyone, display their object, read the Bible passage and then read their one sentence statement.

Make a list

In small groups, share your understandings of the nature of the Kingdom of God and list the findings of all groups on a large sheet of paper or using an overhead projector.

3. For expressing attitudes, beliefs, opinions

Fill a 'treasure chest'

Ask groups to think about other objects they would like to put into the 'treasure chest' which show what the Kingdom of God is like. Have them prepare a statement about this chosen object beginning 'The Kingdom of God is like… because…' Then have each group in turn bring their object (or a drawing of it) to the 'treasure chest' and read this statement to everyone.

A group mural

Place a large sheet of newsprint headed 'The Kingdom of God is like…' on a wall. Ask everyone to draw, write or paste their own conclusion to the sentence on the wall using either a Bible image or some other image which they have chosen. Provide a number of crayons so that several people can work on the mural at one time. Some may prefer to cut

words or pictures from papers or magazines to paste on the mural; others may prefer to do their work on smaller pieces of paper and later attach it to the mural.

4. For celebrating faith and life

A litany

Replace all the objects both biblical and those prepared by group members back into the 'treasure chest'. Have people come to the 'treasure chest' and take one out, saying, 'The Kingdom of God is like…' after which everyone can pray, 'Your kingdom come, O Lord.' People may be able to keep some of the objects as a reminder.

Poems

Write poems expressing some of the joys of belonging to God's Kingdom.

5. For helping persons move into Christian discipleship

Sharing insights

What does belonging to the Kingdom of God mean? If we belong to God's Kingdom, what must we be like? Share your thoughts in small groups — especially the insights you have gained today.

A service project

Plan a service project for your small group or local church to undertake to show that God rules in the lives of people.

Activities about the local church heritage

These activities would be used in relation to a celebration of a church anniversary or thanksgiving day.

1. For deepening relationships with other people

Memories

Ask everyone to take a piece of paper and on it draw a picture of their earliest memory of the local church. Then have everyone move silently around the room looking at the drawings. After a while allow time for people to talk to one another about the drawings.

Name cards

On a piece of paper about 150 x 80 mm, ask people to write their name in large bold letters. Ask people to think about the local church and on various spaces around their name to write down or draw

- a worship service or sermon they particularly remember

- the names of two or three people who meant a lot to them (minister, elder, deacon, Sunday school teacher, member of the congregation…)

- the happiest time they remember

- the saddest time they remember.

Then allow time for everyone to share what they have written down or drawn.

2. For exploring facts, ideas, meanings

A memorabilia display

Ask people beforehand to try to bring to the program an item associated with the history of your local church. They could bring their baptismal or marriage certificate, an order of service, a photograph… Display the items brought. Also display old minute books, baptismal registers, marriage registers, visitor's books, pictures of previous ministers, historic liturgical items, memorial plaques… You could also invite some of the older members to talk about some of the items. In small groups share together something about the history of your church which you discovered that you didn't know before or memories of people or events which the display stirred.

A time line

Mount a long sheet of newsprint on a wall. Mark dates along the sheet from the earliest days of your local church until the present.

Then ask everyone to help fill in the history of the church by writing or drawing on the sheet. This could be done by having people refer to a display (as above) for information or from their own memories. Emphasise that the events should include items like 'I first came to this church — Jim'; 'Our wedding day — Bev and Col'; 'I was baptised — Anne' as well as landmarks like the laying of the foundation stone and so on.

3. For expressing attitudes, beliefs and opinions

Looking forward

Ask people to draw pictures of aspects of your local church as they hope to see it in five or ten years time. Display the pictures for all to see. If you made a time line earlier, you may wish to allow space on the line for drawings or descriptions of people's hopes for the local church.

Completing sentences

Duplicate a number of incomplete sentences on a sheet and ask people to fill them in. Use sentences such as

- I like our church because…

- Our church would be improved by…

- The most interesting parts of our history for me are…

Allow people time to share as much of their sentences as they wish.

Writing a history book

Take a A4 size paper and fold it in two. On the first inside page ask people to draw (or write) about what seems to them to be the most significant **past event** from the local church history. Use the second page for the best thing about the local church **now.** The back page can be their dreams or visions for what the local church can be in the **future** together with a statement 'To help this dream come true I will…' Complete the book by designing a cover including an emblem or slogan about the local church. This activity could also be done in small groups using a larger piece of paper or by asking small groups to do one page only and stapling all the pages together.

4. For celebrating faith and life

A set of banners

Make a set of past-present-future banners to display in worship.

Write prayers

Individually or in small groups write three one-sentence prayers — thanksgiving for the past, confession for failures and help for the future. Display all the prayers on a large prayer poster for all to see.

Put on a play

Ask small groups of 6-8 people to make up a short play from information available in a memorabilia display. Then dress up and put on the plays. (You may wish to select suitable events for the plays beforehand.)

Write a hymn

Choose a hymn and ask small groups to write a new verse for it which celebrates your local church's story. It will be best to choose the same simple tune for all groups though some keen people may like to try a new verse to 'For all the saints…'

5. For helping people move into Christian discipleship

A 'going-on' path

Using a path outside the door of your church or a long piece of newsprint to form a carpet, ask everyone to trace around their footprints (using chalk on the path) with the prints going out from the church. Then ask people to write on their footprints one or two things they will do to help the church to go on into the future.

Plan a thanksgiving service

Speak to your minister and plan together a thanksgiving service for the life and witness of those members of your congregation who have given 50 years or more of service to God and his church. Research the facts carefully and type them on to a card or attractive notelet or pamphlet as a tribute. Complete the card with the words 'For the life and witness of… thanks be to God'.

Send an invitation to the people you are honouring and to their friends. Follow the service with a morning tea.

You could pay tribute to the life of these people in a 'This is your life' format or tell of their life using a Hebrews chapter 11 format.

Activities about the Exodus or going on a journey

1. For deepening relationships

Talk in two's or three's about a **journey** people have recently been on. What things did they take? How much planning did it take? If all participants have not been away then they could listen to the stories of other people.

Look at the words of 'Morning town ride'

This is a song from the original 'Seekers' group. Talk in small groups about what is suggested by the words.

Action game

'I went to Paris' is a game about going on a holiday to Paris. Each person in a circle tells what they bought and then repeats the purchases made by each preceding player. e.g. I went to Paris and I bought a pair of scissors. Person 2: I went to Paris and I bought a bicycle and a pair of scissors. Person 3: I went to Paris and I bought some eggs, a bicycle and a pair of scissors.

2. For exploring facts meaning

Background Biblical material

Exodus chapters 1-11, specific help to be taken from Exodus 12:1-39 and 16:1-26.

Exodus means departure and refers to the central event in Israel's history — the departure of the people of Israel from Egypt where they had been slaves.

Take part in a biblical simulation:

Exodus

by Mary-Ruth Marshall

The purpose of this game is to help players experience something of the drama and excitement of the Exodus experience. A secondary purpose is to learn some facts about the Exodus, and gain some information about life at that time.

Materials needed

Bible for each player.
Copies of the master list of things to take — one copy for each player.
Resource books such as atlas, life in Bible times, etc.
Pencil for each player; paper.

Playing the game

1. Set the scene by reminding players of the background of the Exodus experience. Starting with Joseph's trip to Egypt, trace the life of the Hebrew people in Egypt. Describe Moses' call and his confrontations with Pharaoh. Mention the Passover experience.

2. Maintain an attitude of excitement and expectancy as you tell the players that they have 20 minutes to decide what 15 items they will take on the Exodus trip. To help them decide they have these resources:

● Exodus chapters 1-11 (background)

● Exodus 12:1-39 and 16:1-26 (to be read for specific help)

● master list of possible things to take.

Remind them that they have only 20 minutes before departure time. Answer any questions within that 20 minute period.

3. At the end of 20 minutes stop the listing process. (It is helpful to announce the time at 10, 5, 3, 2 and 1 minute intervals.) Divide the group into 'families' of 5-6 members. Give them the following instructions:

● You are a family of at least three generations (no roles assigned, but that must be taken into consideration).

● You have 30 minutes to decide on the list of 15 items you as a family will take.

● Your list must consist of items which you can transport in some way.

● You must agree on the list, using any agreement means except voting.

● A winning family will be determined by a points system which includes bringing those things the Bible says you **must** bring, those things the Bible says you **did** bring, and those things on which you agree as a family.

34

4. Begin the family decision process. Announce the time at 15, 5 and 1 minute periods. Bring this stage to a close.

5. Ask the families to report, entering their scores on a large sheet of paper. The scoring is as follows:

3 points for each article or category mentioned which they were obliged or told by God to take (ask for proof texts),

2 points for each article or category the Bible says they took,

1 point for each other article on which the group reaches consensus.

6. Declare the team with the most points the winning family. It might be appropriate to give a 'reward' such as dried fruit, unleavened bread, etc.

Master list of possible things to take

ointment	musical instruments (2)	salt
cosmetics	goats (2?)	herbs
garments (3)	sheep, lambs (2)	staff (2)
turban	cattle (2)	tents (2)
extra cloak	extra sandals	dough (3)
extra coat	pestle and mortar	water
wine	olives	storage jars
honey	carpentry tools	cooking pots
gold and silver	Joseph's bones (2)	millstones
jewellery (3)	scarlet cloth	tentlamp (2)
extra tunics	wooden cart	oil
sandals (2)	kneading bowl (3)	wooden chest
goatskin bags and bottles	flour	loom
bed rolls or mats	grain	dried fruits

NOTE: The figures 2 or 3 in brackets following some of the listed items are for guidance in scoring. They should not, of course, be included on the list issued to participants. The 2 or 3 points should only be awarded if the group is able to show an appropriate biblical reference. Extra points may be given for any other items for which players can give a proof text.

(Reprinted from *On the Move* Issue 6 November 1974)

Weekend camp

For a weekend camp you could actually take your group on a journey. Some of the items on the master list could be easily provided. Others would have to be imagined. You may even be fortunate enough to find a 'Red Sea'.

3. For expressing attitudes, beliefs and opinions

Questions for discussion:

1. Did you ever get the feeling of what it was like to be a part of that hasty Exodus? What were your feelings?

2. What did you learn about the Exodus experience which you hadn't known before or had forgotten?

3. Did you see this game experience in any way related to your own life?

4. How did your family reach agreement about which items to take? Were there any strong disagreements?

5. At what point in the game did you most feel understanding of or sympathy for the Hebrews at the time of Exodus?

6. What is the chief learning you gained from this game?

Expressing the Exodus experience

Have available paints, clay and scrap materials. Invite people to express their Exodus experience in whichever way they choose, using some of the material available.

Talk about your feelings, the learnings as outlined in questions above.

4. For celebrating faith and life

In your simulated family groups find or make a symbol that shows an understanding of the feelings of the Hebrews at the time of Exodus.

If your learning event is before worship, then continue the journey of the Hebrews into worship. Take a symbol or expression of your learning and explain it to the congregation.

5. For helping persons move into Christian discipleship

Think about your family

and what you know of its history. Talk in two's and three's about how it feels to be part of that family. Small children could draw their parents and grandparents, aunts, uncles and cousins.

Think about the Exodus

and the long line of God's people that you are part of.

Write a prayer of thanks

for the Christian heritage. Children could provide the illustrations. The prayer could be used at the conclusion of the session.

Activities about building community

1. For deepening relationships

Who am I?

As people arrive invite them to take a card and write or draw as many answers to 'Who am I?' as is possible in three minutes (or the time you have), e.g. child, kind, cricket fan… Then choose four or five of the most apt descriptions and write on the reverse side for others to read.

A previous community

Bring and share something from a past community e.g. photograph of people involved in a particular activity, baptism certificate etc.

In groups of three of four talk about what you have brought.

2. For exploring facts, ideas, meanings

Read the story *The Bunyip of Berkeley's Creek* (see page 43). There are no page numbers so pause at 'No one saw him and no one spoke to him…'

Talk to the person next to you about how the Bunyip felt. Have you ever felt like the Bunyip?

Form a community

If you have completed 'Who am I?' from section 1, invite people to move around and read each other's cards. Choose two or three people willing to form a community with you. Base your choice on something another person can give or something you need. Young children are likely to stay with a parent. Briefly discuss what each person brings to the community and what each person needs from the community.

Decide on a symbol of acceptance for your community

to be used later in the session.

Anti-community

Invite each community to choose a representative who is then asked to leave the room for a short time, and not talk to anybody.

The remaining members of each group are to play a quiet game, e.g. hangman. When the representatives return the members are not to talk to them.

They may show them the paper they are playing on and a sign that reads 'please find another group' and continue their game.

After a few minutes invite the representatives back to join the communities and to talk.

The leader needs to allow enough time for adequate discussion to take place. There may be some strong feelings that need to be expressed. The leader needs to conclude this section by reflecting on the feelings of both the representatives and other members in creating anti-community.

Acceptance

The Bunyip story is completed. The leader invites the original communities to re-form by using the symbol of acceptance chosen in an earlier step.

In small groups

Think about the different communities of which you are a part. List them. Are there some groups or communities you would like to be part of, but for various reasons cannot be? Talk about this for a few minutes.

Write, draw, cut and paste

what is good about these communities and what makes belonging difficult.

3. For expressing attitudes, beliefs and opinions

What are the marks of a Christian community?

Choose five readers to read the passage from 1 Cor. 12:12-27. You will need a narrator and a foot v. 15, ear v. 16, an eye v. 21a, head v. 21b.

Express the concept through

a. Making the various parts of the body and fitting them together.

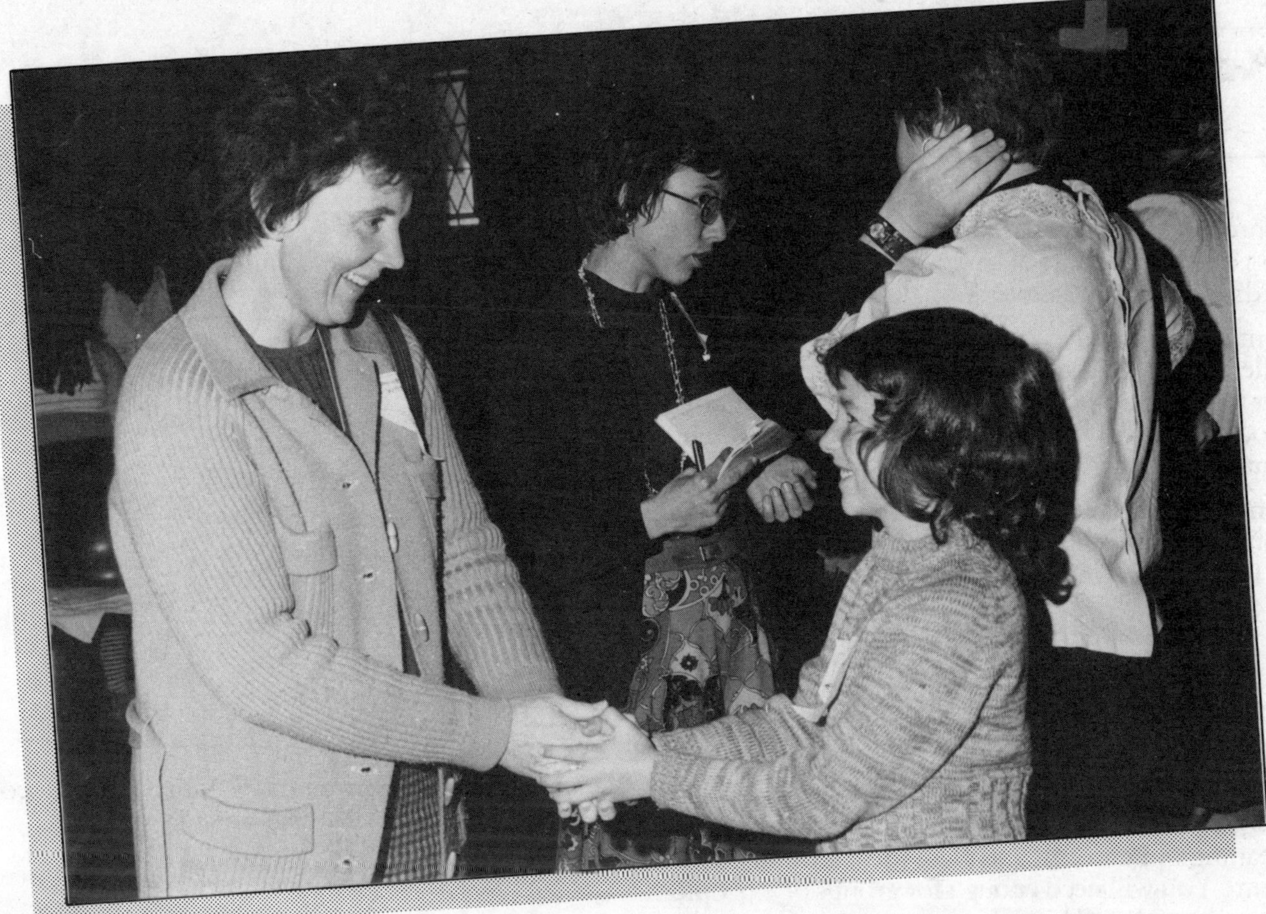

or

b. Discovering the various parts/groups of your congregation and putting them together as a whole. You could do this through first listing the nurturing/ learning/caring groups/activities that your congregation is expressing. Are there any gaps? If so what would be the first step in filling those gaps or needs?

4. For celebrating faith and life

Write a prayer

for those who are alone and lonely. Think of individuals known to you. What are their needs? Is there some way you might help?

Ask each small community

from section two to offer themselves in some way to the larger community. Each group could create a symbol, movement, Bible reading, a statement or thought and offer it to the larger community.

Write a litany

commencing with 'We thank you that we belong together'.

Create movement

to 'The Body' from *Australian Psalms* by Bruce Prewer. This could be done in a small or large group. (See page   for further help)

5. For helping people move into Christian discipleship

Covenant

to continue to find ways for 'The Body' to better understand the diversity within it.

Send a deputation

to your governing body offering to do some work in the area of the 'gap' as outlined in 3b above.

Take home your symbol of acceptance

as a reminder of what it means to be part of a 'community'.

Plan

with your minister to present in worship the symbols of your involvement in your community.

Pentecost was a Jewish Harvest Festival, a celebration of the first fruits of harvest which was held 50 days after the Passover.

Pentecost marked the end of a period of waiting, of reflection, of doubt and despair. It took the disciples out from seclusion and into the conflicts of the public proclamation of the Gospel. They went out as men transformed, with a new sense of power and courage.

Pentecost is a day when we celebrate the gift of God's Spirit to those who would proclaim the Good news of Jesus to the whole world.

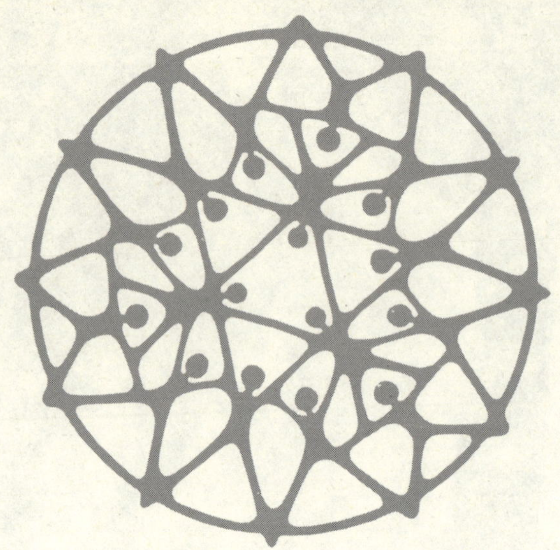

1. For deepening relationships with other people

Name cards

Provide some Bible dictionaries or copies of the meaning of Pentecost and place them around the room. You will need enough for groups of 4 people to work on. Provide cards or strong paper approximately 12 x 10 cm, textas and pens.

As people arrive ask them to write their name on one side of the cards in bold print.

Then invite them in small groups of no more than 4 people to discover the meaning of the word Pentecost and to write it on the back of their name cards.

Picture viewing

Provide a display of large pictures/posters of the fruits of the spirit. Be sure to include some that speak to children and young people: love, joy, peace, patience, kindness, goodness, faithfulness, humility, self control.

As people arrive arrange them in small groups of up to 4 people of mixed ages and invite them to look at the pictures and posters and talk briefly about their meaning.

See 2. for further exploration of the pictures.

2. Exploring facts, ideas, meanings

Refer to the Bible passages Acts 2:1-11 and Galatians 5:22, 23. Refer again to the fruits of the Spirit and invite those present to stand beside a poster or picture of their choice and talk with the other people about why they chose that particular poster.

Questions could include

● What attracted you to this particular picture or poster?

● Why is this gift important to you?

● Share an experience of this gift in your life.

● Think about the times in your life when it has been difficult to act in this way.

Adults will need to allow children to express themselves. They will have times they can identify but they may need a little help in expressing themselves.

Very young children could look at the pictures, tell why they chose that picture and then do some drawing.

Telling the Bible story in several languages

If you have people of other nationalities, ask them to dress in clothes of their homeland and have each person read the Bible passages in their own language — all at the same time. **This is not to demonstrate speaking in tongues,** but the diversity and unity within the Spirit. In small groups talk about the experience of the Bible being read in so many languages.

Pentecost

'Pentecost' from *Australian Psalms* by Bruce Prewer
provides 10 verses of rich symbolism for exploration.
New Zealand readers can replace a few words to suit
local geography. Depending on the size of your
group you may wish to divide the group and allocate
one verse to each group. Take time to visualise the
images expressed by Bruce Prewer. Your own images
of Pentecost could be presented to the total group.

3. For expressing attitudes, beliefs, opinions

Think again of the fruits of the Spirit

In small groups of adults and young people, talk
about the fruits of the Spirit you find more difficult
to express. Why do you think this is so? Make a
poster or collage to express this. What might help
you to develop this particular gift?

Create a symbol

that speaks to you of one of the gifts of the spirit.

4. For celebrating faith and life

Write a prayer and reflection

beginning with

- The Spirit produces love...

- Make a statement about love... and so on
through all the gifts.

- End with a response commencing with 'Father by
your Spirit...'

Write a message

about each of the fruits of the Spirit, place each one in
a balloon, fill them with helium gas and send them
heavenwards to land we know not where!

Sing together

the hymn 'God sends us his Spirit' (no. 324 *The
Australian Hymn Book/With One Voice*).

5. For helping people move into Christian discipleship

Make a contract

with another person to explore further the gifts you
find most difficult in your own life.

Exchange your name card

as a reminder of another person — and the diversity
of the people who have received the Spirit of God
and the unity of all people under God.

Use one of the posters

as a talking point with someone not involved in this
learning event.

Activities about The Trinity

The Trinity speaks to us of ways in which we know God

1. For deepening relationships with other people

'Tri' words

On arrival give each person a small card and pen/pencil. Ask them to write down all the 'tri' words they can think of.

Talk in two's or three's about their meaning.

Before the event

Draw a triangle on the front of the 'Order of Service' or on a card if you don't have an order.

Use small different coloured stickers placed in different corners of the triangle to indicate how to form groups. When people have found their partners, talk about the triangle and its meaning for them.

2. For exploring facts, ideas, meanings

'Trinity'

'Trinity' from *Australian Prayers* by Bruce Prewer provides opportunity to think about the times when one has lost faith in the goodness of creation… when one has lost faith in Jesus… When were those times and what happened to help restore your faith in either of these areas of life? In the second part of the prayer think about the words of love and forgiveness. Who are some of the people and situations where love and forgiveness have been shown. For primary age children the questions would need to be rephrased and may go something like, 'can you think of times when things did not seem to be going right in your world?'

'Ice — Water — Steam'

Have the leader place some chunks of ice into a fireproof container and heat over a portable gas jet. Talk about what happens. All three, ice, water and steam, are part of the same thing.

3. For expressing attitudes, beliefs and opinions

Refer back to the triangle

Find your partners as per the coloured circles. Using the words, *Trinity, Father, Son* and *Spirit,* have the small groups make a large letter that will fit into a poster (or posters) or a wall mural.

Depending on the number of groups, you may need some groups to make more than one letter, or, if you have a very large group, then two posters could be made.

4. For celebrating faith and life

'Father Son and Holy Spirit'
by John McRae

O God our Father,
power behind earth and sea,
great architect of the universe,
love that flows out to me.

Lord God, could you be man,
with our weakness, crying and hungry and dying?
Jesus you showed that God can come
to walk with me.

Holy Spirit, ever with us,
gentle fire of love,
bringing hope, joy, faith, peace,
making us one.

Say together responsively
the prayer 'Trinity' by Bruce Prewer (see 2. above)
or

Psalm 8 as a statement of the glory of God and the dignity of people.

5. For helping people move into Christian discipleship

Hang the banner

or posters that were made out of words of the trinity

in your church or other prominent place.

Make a small reminder of the poster to take home.

Say together

the *Statement of Belief* from the United Church of Canada (see page 17).

Activities about Family

1. For deepening relationships with other people

Small groups

In small groups as people arrive talk about these questions

● What are the things that make us happy to be in a family?

● What does being part of an extended family mean to you? If you are not part of an extended family then talk about what you think you miss by not having that experience.

● What are the qualities for which you are thankful in your family?

Small children might like to draw something about their family.

As people arrive

give each one a flower

Browsing time

As part of your planning time gather pictures of different family models, e.g. nuclear family, single parent family, extended family, mixed nationalities. Place these around the wall. On arrival, invite participants to browse through the pictures.

2. For exploring facts, ideas, meanings

Family definitions

Ask for definitions of the word family — gather as many as you can. As you hear the definitions invite people to come and model them.

Invite people to choose activities

in their family groups and form simulated families where there are singles and children present.

How well do you know your mum or dad?

See how accurate you are on these statements.

MUM She loves…
        She likes to buy…
        Dad thinks she's…
        She's good at…

DAD When he comes home…
        I appreciate his…
        After tea he…
        He enjoys………on T.V.

Add more of your own.

Future families

Help the teenagers discover what kind of family they want to have. What ideas and ideals do they have? Are they any different to the ideals of their parents?

Provide resources to help people discover the strengths and weaknesses of family life, e.g. good communication patterns, love, caring, unhappiness, breakdown. Use newspaper cuttings, pictures, statistics etc.

Frieze

Build up a frieze that shows the complex nature of family life.

3. For expressing attitudes, beliefs and opinions

Make a family time line

beginning with Mum and Dad meeting. Think about the highs and lows for all family members.

Make a collage

on the theme 'Families have the stength'. This assumes families do have the strength. Use magazines, scissors, scraps, etc., that say something about the theme. Add drawings and writings. Be satisfied if it is a realistic collage, not a romantic dream as portrayed by television.

4. For celebrating faith and life

Stand in a circle

You will need a ball of wool. The leader begins by hanging on to the end. Throw the ball of wool to a person, name them and say something you like about them. This person hangs on to part of the wool and then throws the ball to someone else and so on until every person is included and all are attached to each other.

Family rituals

Ask each family or simulated family group to share a ritual that is important to them. Provide opportunity for these to be shared. If time allows choose one suitable for the large group.

5. For helping people move into Christian discipleship

Take home the results of your activities.

Think pray and celebrate

Think about your family. Is there anything you would like to change that would improve your life together?

Write a prayer of thanks for each member of your family.

Write a prayer for other families.

Celebrate the differences in families discovered in section 2.

The use of stories in all-age learning

Last week I attended a seminar and much of the teaching for the day was done through the use of stories. Today in the supermarket I met a friend and we swapped stories — to catch up on what had happened since last we met. Our days are filled with stories; stories of the day's activities that we tell at the dinner table, stories that come through the media and those that come through books.

The use of stories in a learning program is important. We are used to telling the stories of the Bible, but there are many modern stories that can be used as well.

Choosing appropriate stories can be the most difficult part. (See below for some you can use.)

The use of stories enables the listeners to make their own connections at the point of meaning for themselves.

How to use stories

What is the point of the story? Or to put it another way, what is the theme you want to build on?

How will you do this? Will the story be the main learning? If not what else do you need to add?

How will you tell the story? Will you tell it in part? (See 'Activities about building community', page 36.) Will you tell it in your own words? Is it better read as it is?

The following are some stories that have been used in all-age events.

THE BUNYIP OF BERKELEY'S CREEK   by Jenny Wagner and Pictures by Ron Brooks, Kestrel and Puffin, 1974. 'One night, something very large and muddy heaved itself on to the bank of Berkeley's Creek. "What am I?", it murmured. "What do I look like?"… The Bunyip set off to find out for himself.' Used in this manual under 'Activities about building community' page

GRASSHOPPER ON THE ROAD   by Arnold Lobel, World's Work Ltd., Surrey, 1979. 'Grasshopper wanted to go on a journey. "I will find a road," he said, "I will follow that road wherever it goes" ' …and so grasshopper continued many journeys each with its own theme.

HOPE FOR THE FLOWERS   words and pictures by Trina Paulus, Paulist Press, New York, 1972. This is a tale partly about life — partly about revolution and lots about hope. A tale of a caterpillar who has trouble becoming what he really is. 'It's like myself — like us.' So writes the author and rightly so.

AUSTRALIAN PSALMS and AUSTRALIAN PRAYERS by Bruce Prewer, both Lutheran Publishing House, Adelaide, 1979 and 1983, are excellent resources and referred to under several titles in the 'Activities' section of this book.

Most of the material in Bruce Prewer's books is suitable for places outside Australia. In those instances where there is a particularly Australian reference it is possible to replace it with other references.

Other sources

a) your own bookshelves

b) libraries and librarians

c) any friends who work with children or young people

d) your nearest bookshop.

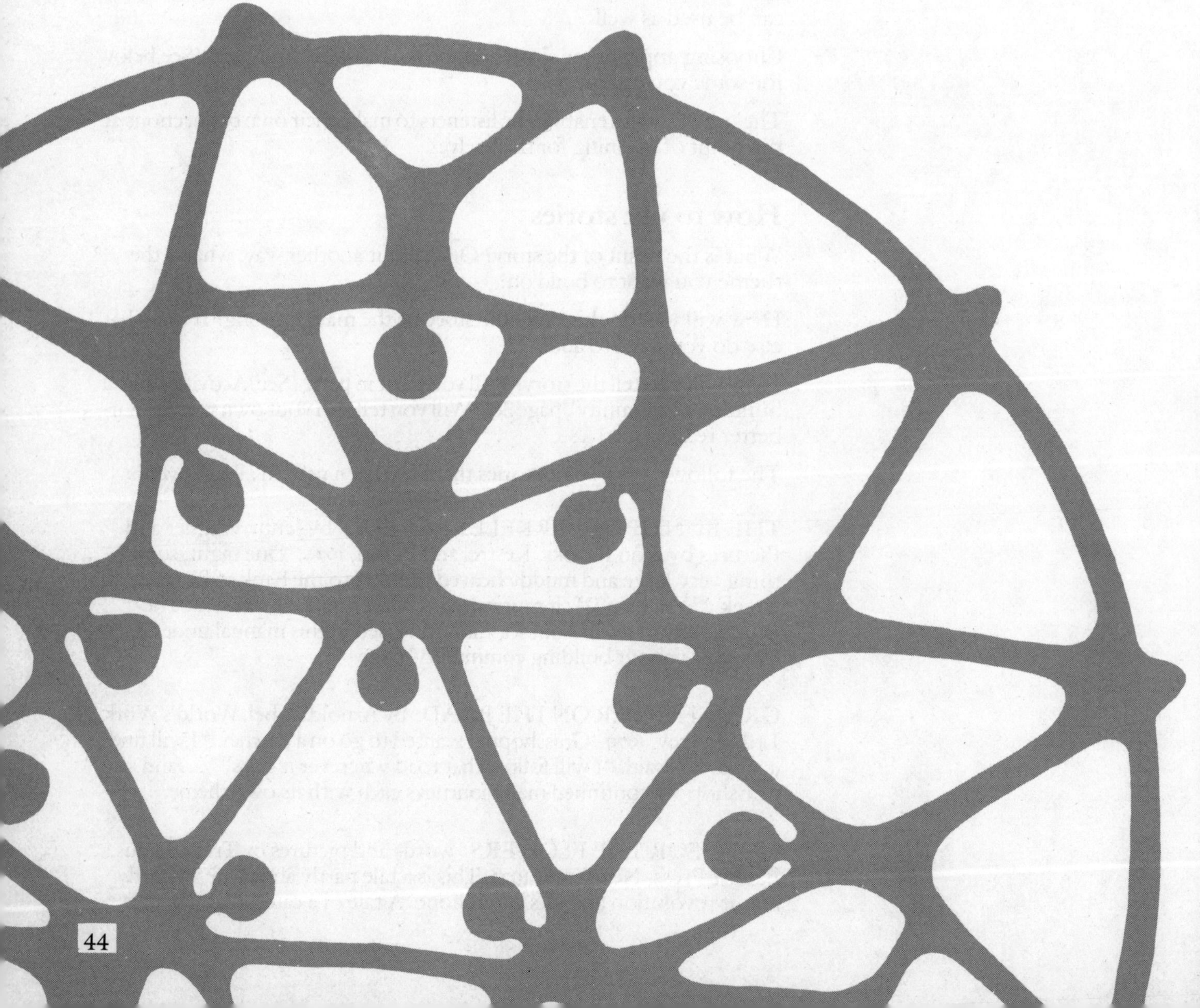

Live better — live simply

Some Ideas

● As people arrive ask them to work with a partner (people who can't yet read and write easily have an older partner). List the things you have around the house that your grandparents did not have, e.g. electric stove, motor mower. Then mark which is essential and which could be done without or shared with another family.

● Prepare Bible readings — divide your group into small groups of mixed ages. Each group to answer briefly on a wall sheet a couple of questions and prepare a Bible reading using a narrator and a mime of tableau (living picture) to illustrate its meaning.

Acts 3:1-10 How would you feel if you were always needing charity to get by? What did the crippled man really want? What do poor people and disadvantaged people today really want?

Luke 12:15-21 What did Jesus mean us to learn from this story? At what point did the rich man 'go wrong'?

Luke 16:19-31 What was Jesus' purpose in telling this vivid fable?

Mark 10:20-31 Why did Jesus ask the rich man to give away everything?

Have each group show their tableau to the whole group.

Stewardship

Bible reading
Matthew 25:14-30

Aim
To think of stewardship as a way of life.

Some ideas

● Act out the story from Matthew 25:14-30. Use different size bags of jelly beans — enough for all present. Tell each other how it felt to be in charge of different size bags.

● List comments from all ages about times when they have been given an opportunity to do something with a talent or gift. What had they done with it?

● What talents/gifts is each person able to identify in themselves/in others? How can these be encouraged?

● Can you offer a talent or gift for your own use and for the good of the faith community? How can you encourage the gift of another person?

The world into which Jesus came

Some ideas

● Using maps look at where the Roman empire stretched. What was civilisation at that time? What was the character of the different parts of the known world? Was it educated, if so in what ways? Look at the area where Jesus was born. Which parts were at peace and which parts were tense or at war? What about the place of the Jews — who was King? What happened to Herod over the years? What happened after Herod died? What were the feelings about the hoped for Messiah? Use picture, maps and people who have visited in that area.

Preparing for Christmas

Theme
To raise awareness of the differences in lifestyle of people who **have** against people who **have not.**

Some ideas
(People living away from centres of population will find this idea is not suitable for them.)

Divide the group into small car sized groups of all ages.

● Think about the places in your area that will have some of the following: special schools, migrant hostel, church or state homes for boys/girls, and reception centres for children; contrasts in housing, contrast in schools — private/state, inner city, or 'new' areas; the growing number of Sunday markets in some parts of Australia.

● Drive past some or all of the institutions and places listed in the previous paragraph. Pause at each to think about: the purpose of this institution? Who uses the facilities? Does this institution mean poverty? What is poverty?

Add more questions of your own.

● On your return list your comments on newsprint paper large enough to be easily read by the rest of the group. Small children could draw some of the places they saw on their travels.

● Think about Christmas in your family. If you have accurate facts to compare your Christmas with that of people in the places you drove to, then do so.

● Are there any changes or additions you wish to make to your preparation for the Christmas season?

Holy week

Learning centres

The events of Holy week lend themselves to be taught and experienced through 'learning centres'. If you have enough rooms then the following could be a very good learning activity for you.

Choose the events of Holy week for which you have space and leadership. If you are not able to enact all of Holy week then be sure to create a bridge between the events you choose.

1. The Triumphant entry

The Sunday worship service may be an appropriate place to remember Jesus and his entry into Jerusalem. Some places have even managed a **real** donkey. A very dramatic way to demonstrate the triumphant entry to your local community.

2. The Passover and Last Supper

You do not need a very large room to house tables for the Passover. There are pictures from which you can copy the decor of the room. It is likely that you will have more people than the original twelve disciples. This need not detract from the learning experience.

3. The Garden of Gethsemane

If you have time and the resources, painting a backdrop of the garden adds enormously to the general effect. (Even if your numbers are limited, don't accidentally choose a female Judas and a male Jesus both of youthful age and risk them dissolving into laughter.)

4. High court and courtyard

Into the fourth room arrange a high court on one side and the courtyard where Peter is seen, and where he denies Jesus. There are good sound effects records available with a cock crowing. Some of the music from *Jesus Christ Superstar* adds some variety, as does showing slides of the trial of Jesus.

5. Mount of Olives

The stage of a hall makes a good Mount of Olives where Jesus is crucified.

6. Empty tomb

A small room or spare corner can house an empty tomb made from lots of brown paper covering a table.

This way of learning helps people to get into the shoes of the people and events at the time of Jesus.

More 'topics'

There are other situations and events that lend themselves to this way of learning. They include: Paul's journey and events that took place in certain cities or towns e.g. Jerusalem and Bethlehem. A good Bible dictionary and concordance will help, and of course your minister will be an excellent resource person.

Salt of the earth

Matthew 5:13-16

Some ideas

● Before the event, prepare as many cards as you are likely to have participants. On each small card write one word taken from the Bible passage Matthew 5:13-16, e.g. 'salt', 'all', 'mankind'. Have people talk in two's and three's about the word and their card.

● Bring enough scones for each person to have one half scone made with salt and one half made without salt. Talk in small groups about the difference between the two pieces of scone.

● Spend a few minutes thinking about how you see yourself as salt in your relationships. What do I need for myself to be the 'salt' with my friends. What effect does being 'salt' have on your family and friends?

Include young people and children. If they have tasted the difference between the scones, they will understand what is being asked of them.

● Make a collage on the effect of being 'salt' in your relationships, in your school or in your workplace.

An Emmaus walk

Themes
New Life
Turning points

Some ideas

● Each person to bring some flowers to put at the foot of the cross. New life, colour, hope, are all evident around the cross.

● Dramatise the story, then use these questions to draw it out: Why were they feeling this way? What were their feelings when the third person joined them? What were the turning points of the journey? What were the feelings of Cleopas and his friend then? The key points for you are...?

● Bring back something that represents new life

● Go on an 'Emmaus Walk'. Choose someone you would like to know better. Introduce yourselves, talk about all the things that have happened recently, the sad as well as the happy. Share what Easter means to you. Chat about the feelings that might have been expressed by the disciples and Jesus in the events of Holy week. In what ways do we experience these same feelings today? Share briefly.

● At the conclusion each person takes back some flowers (not the ones you brought). They symbolise the new life, colour and hope that is part of your life as a Christian.

Elijah

1 Kings 18:41 - 19:12

Themes

To acknowledge the times when we feel like running away from situations.

To discover what the story of Elijah has to say to us.

To discover how we can be helped to face the issues that cause us concern, anxiety etc.

1 Kings 18:41 - 19:12   'Bible Stories' as retold by David Kossoff.

Elijah was a man with a deep sense of the presence of God with him — so what happened to make him run away?

Some ideas

● Act out the main point of the Elijah story.

● Identify some situations that people may have run from or wanted to run from — act out one or two of them.

● Act out different ways that might help someone face a situation.

● Name some people who have stood firm in the face of difficulty.

● Sing 'One more step along the world I go' (Sidney Carter) and/or 'God gives his people strength' (Medical Mission Sisters from *Joy is like the rain*).

Choose a person

A very useful way to learn about Bible characters.

Women of the Bible

● Choose the women whose shoes you would like to be in for a time, e.g. Ruth, Naomi, Mary, Martha, Mary Magdalene.

● Using Bible dictionaries, Bible atlases, pictures, 'Bible stories as retold by David Kossoff', assemble information so you have enough for each person in your group to choose one Bible character.

● When your group has chosen their particular person invite all those who chose Ruth to join a group together … all those who chose Naomi … etc. If you have a large group you may need several groups on the one person.

● Encourage the people present, including children, to become that person for the next hour or so.

Find out all you can about that person, when she lived, who her friends were, her relationship to Jesus (if New Testament), what the world she lived in was like. What was the setting for the story? What appeals to you about that person?

● Find a way or ways to introduce that person to the total group. Some ways of doing this could include — a time line, acting of the story, tell your story beginning with: 'My name is Ruth, I lived …'

Alternative

During Lent choose several people of the Bible (including some of the disciples) who were important to the Easter story. Use the method as outlined for **Women of the Bible** above.

Other groupings of Bible characters

Kings and prophets

Meeting the twelve disciples

The people of Advent — Elizabeth, Mary, Joseph, Herod, a census taker.

Mark 12:28-34

This is an old Jewish method of studying the Bible. It was used to 'feel' and 'understand' the passage.

Some ideas

This method is only appropriate with children who are able to read.

Each person walks around the room reading the passage out loud. Do this three times in all and quite loudly.

At the conclusion of the third time sit down in pairs (adult and young person) and relate the passage to each other in turn. Then tell the story in your own words to communicate the meaning as though to another person who hasn't heard this passage before.

Write on the board the people who were present and any other background material.

● Dramatise the passage, drawing out the feelings of the people and groups there. How did they react to what Jesus said?

● Dramatise the passage making and using puppets instead of people.

● What does it mean to love the Lord your God with . . . all your heart, all your soul, all your mind, all your strength and to love your neighbour as yourself?

● With which is it harder to love God — your heart, soul, mind or strength? Why do you think this is so?

How much is it possible to love your neighbour without loving yourself?

Being Christian at school, at work and at home

Some ideas

● 'Our Work' from *Australian Psalms* by Bruce Prewer. Read the psalm together or have it read. Think about your own work, school or home, whichever place you identify as being 'work'. Do you place yourself anywhere in that psalm just at present?

● Prepare a poster or time line showing your work (defined as above). Show how you are Christian in that place, doing that job.

● Invite three or four people to prepare a short story about 'Being Christian at work'. (It's a great way to get to know people as well!)

● Look at the hymn 'Son of the Father, Jesus, Lord and slave' (No. 184 *The Australian Hymn Book/With One Voice*). What does this hymn have to say about being Christian at work or school? You might write another verse for this hymn.

● Luke 10:25-37 The parable of the Good Samaritan is a familiar story. What does that say about the time when you saw someone who was . . .?

Design for a 'Christian lifestyle'

Some ideas

● Read the Parable of the Rich Fool — Luke 12:13-21 and brainstorm the meaning of the story.

● In small groups assume you have been given twelve months — free from all your normal obligations and restraints.

Now look at the elements which would be necessary for you to incorporate into a complete design for a 'Christian lifestyle'.

Children as well as adults could be involved in drawing or cutting from magazines to build up a picture of what is important for a Christian lifestyle.

Is this different from the one you are already part of? If so how? What changes would you need to make in order to live out that lifestyle? Is there a price? If so, are you prepared to pay that price?

The lost sheep and lost coin

Luke 15:1-7 and Luke 15:8-10

Some ideas

● Read these two stories. What do you notice about the endings of the two stories?

● Pretend you are a Pharisee listening to these parables. You are a religious leader of the day. You feel you have earned a special place with God because of your great learning and the careful way you keep the Law. You feel responsible for making sure that other people keep the Law too.

● How would a Pharisee feel hearing these stories? How do you feel? Share your answers.

OR

Theme
Being lost

Some ideas

● Think about a time when you were lost or knew of someone else who was lost. Share how it felt. Can you remember how it felt to be found?

● Hide some coins around the room and ask people to pretend they belong to each of them and begin a search for the 'lost' money. How did it feel to have to spend time in that way? How did it feel when the coins were eventually found?

New beginnings

Luke 15:11-32

Some ideas

● Think of some new beginnings each person faced recently or will be facing in the future. Children can think of school, brownies, cubs etc.

What feelings do you experience when facing such a new beginning? What will help you face new beginnings?

● Act out the story of the Prodigal son. What new beginnings did each of the characters in the story have to face? What helped them to do it?

● As the story is told paint different colours for each character. What did you discover from that exercise?

Creation

Theme

An affirmation of God as Creator and of the goodness of creation.

Genesis 1.

Some ideas

● Create an exciting room environment with posters from National parks, forestry departments, travel agents and books from your own shelves. Be creative and tape the sound of waves pounding against the sand.

● Spend some time looking around the room. How many colours do you see? Are you reminded of any places you have been to? If so, can you recall the sounds, the odours, the temperature etc.?

● Choose a poster. Stand very still in front of it, imagine you are actually there. What do you see, hear?

Are you more, or less, aware of God in this environment? Why?

● Think about why Christians should be concerned about the environment.

● In small groups look at Matthew 25:31-46, Luke 12:6, Matthew 6:24-34. These readings deal in one way or another with the relationship between man and God and man's responsibility for others and his environment.

If on a camp

Some more ideas

● In small groups go to the beach area (or wherever you are). Make a list as you go, of spontaneous reactions as you crawl, walk, run through, ride over, stand on, wriggle out of, smell, touch, listen to ... your surroundings. When the spontaneous reactions cease, these questions may evoke some more responses: How many sounds do you hear? How many colours do you see? Do you see any life under logs, rocks, etc.?

● Are you more, or less, aware of God in this environment? Why?

● Make a picture by takings rubbings of surfaces in your environment.

● If you have a polaroid camera, take photographs — look for the unusual angles, these may pick up your feelings.

● Sketch or paint some aspect of the environment,

maybe small and in detail, black and white. Produce later in a church magazine.

- Make a plaster cast in sand.

- If you were asked to write a statement about how you see God in this environment, could you do it? Do you feel or sense God in this environment? What is a spiritual environment? Would you like the power to change the environment? Why?

- How do you feel in this environment — at ease, or an intruder? Why? Do you want to return here?

- Sit on the beach and let the sand drift through your fingers. How big or small do you feel?

- Listen to the rhythm of the waves. Does it remind you of anything?

- Read from *Bible stories retold by David Kossoff* the account of Creation.

- Think about how you can show a sense of caring responsibility towards those who follow us in this place.

ONE MORE STEP ALONG THE WORLD I GO

1. One more step along the world I go,
   One more step along the world I go.
   From the old things to the new
   Keep me travelling along with you.
     And it's from the old I travel to the new
     Keep me travelling along with you.

2. Round the corners of the world I turn,
   More and more about the world I learn,
   All the new things that I see
   You'll be looking at along with me.
     And it's from the old I travel to the new
     Keep me travelling along with you.

3. As I travel through the bad and good
    Keep me travelling the way I should.
    Where I see no way to go
    You'll be telling me the way, I know.
        And it's from the old I travel to the new
        Keep me travelling along with you.

4. Keep me singing when the road is rough,
    Give me courage when the world is tough.
    Leap and laugh in all I do,
    Keep me travelling along with you.
        And it's from the old I travel to the new
        Keep me travelling along with you.

5. You are older than the world can be.
    You are younger than the life in me.
    Ever old and ever new,
    Keep me travelling along with you.
        And it's from the old I travel to the new
        Keep me travelling along with you.

                                Sydney Carter

Using the lectionary readings

Another good place to start looking for your theme is the lectionary readings for the day.

The lectionary is a systematic arrangement of key passages of the Bible to be read in public worship over a period of time.

Copies of the lectionary may be obtained from the Joint Board of Christian Education Resources Centre or Christian bookshops.

● Planning is enhanced by the meeting together of a small group of people (hopefully including your minister). A good concordance is also invaluable.

Step 1 — Select your reading.

Step 2 — Explore it for possible themes.

Step 3 — What is the learning(s) you want to convey?

Step 4 — Choose activities that will achieve your goal.

Step 5 — Evaluate.

Hymns

● For example 'Lord of the Dance', No. 183 *The Australian Hymn Book/With One Voice*.

The aim is to explore the meaning of the hymn and create a dance or movement to express its meaning. The method you will use will depend on the size of your group. If you chose 'Lord of the Dance', the whole group could create movement for the chorus and small groups could each take one verse.

● Questions for small groups could include: Read the words of the hymn. What do these words mean for you? What movements suggest themselves?

It is helpful to provide some aids. Lengths of material, various size scarves are very useful.